music is fun!

SELECTIONS FROM

STAR WARS®

FOR RECORDER

W9-AVN-846

CONTENTS

MUSIC BY JOHN WILLIAMS
ARRANGED FOR RECORDER

EXCLUSIVELY DISTRIBUTED BY

 HAL•LEONARD®

Copyright © MMVIII by Alfred Publishing Co., Inc.
All rights reserved. Printed in USA.

Book and Recorder
ISBN-10: 0-7390-5320-5
ISBN-13: 978-0-7390-5320-1

Book
ISBN-10: 0-7390-4245-9
ISBN-13: 978-0-7390-4245-8

About the Recorder

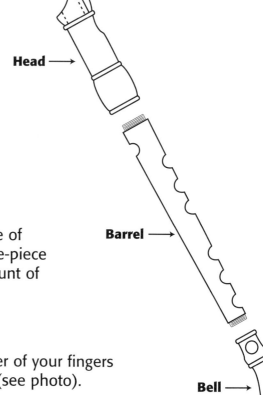

Parts of the Recorder

Although some recorders are made of one single piece, many are made up of three pieces that fit snugly together. The top is called the *head;* the middle is called the *barrel,* and the bottom is called the *bell.* The very top of the head is called the *mouthpiece,* which is the part of the recorder into which you blow.

Care of the Recorder

Each time you finish playing, it is important to run a swab through the recorder to dry all the moisture. A small piece of towel attached to a stick will work well. If you have a three-piece recorder, you may need to occasionally apply a small amount of cork grease to keep the sections from sticking together.

Holding the Recorder

When holding the recorder, it is important to use the center of your fingers to cover each hole, keeping the fingers as flat as possible (see photo). It is not correct to cover the holes with just the tips of the fingers.

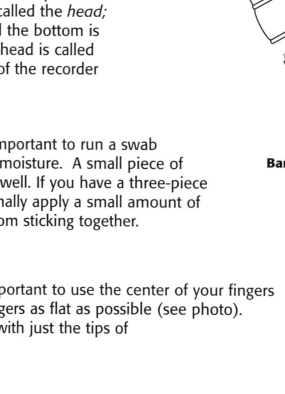

Playing the Recorder

Be sure not to put any more than one-half inch of the mouthpiece into your mouth. Touch the mouthpiece only with your lips, and be sure not to bite the mouthpiece with your teeth. When blowing into the instrument, it is important not to blow too hard. At first, play softly, because this will help you develop control. To begin a note, lightly tap your tongue against the roof of your mouth as if you were saying "tu."

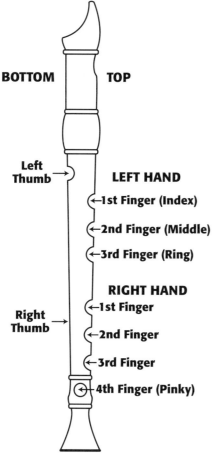

Getting Acquainted with Music

Notes

Notes are used to indicate musical sounds. Some notes are long and others are short.

whole note   o   gets 4 beats

half note   ♩   gets 2 beats

quarter note   ♩   gets 1 beat

eighth note   ♪   gets ½ beat

sixteenth note   ♬   gets ¼ beat

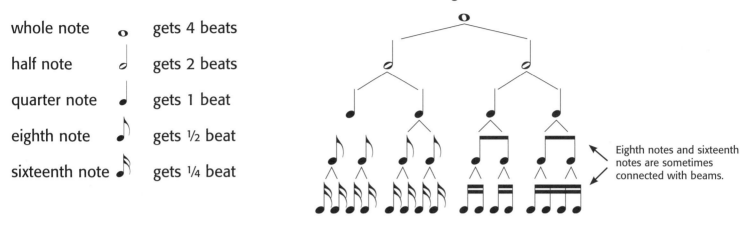

Eighth notes and sixteenth notes are sometimes connected with beams.

When a *dot* follows a note, the length of the note is longer by one half of the note's original length.

dotted half note   ♩.   gets 3 beats

dotted quarter note   ♩.   gets 1½ beats

dotted eighth note   ♪.   gets ¾ beat

Rests

Rests are used to indicate musical silence.

whole rest   ▬   gets 4 beats

half rest   ▬   gets 2 beats

quarter rest   𝄽   gets 1 beat

eighth rest   𝄾   gets ½ beat

sixteenth rest   𝄿   gets ¼ beat

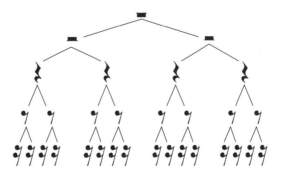

Staff

 Music is written on a *staff* made up of five lines. Between each line there is a space.

line 5 ⟶ _____

line 4 ⟶ _____ ⟵ space 4

line 3 ⟶ _____ ⟵ space 3

line 2 ⟶ _____ ⟵ space 2

line 1 ⟶ _____ ⟵ space 1

In this book, you will see letters above the staff called *chord symbols* that can be played by a friend on another instrument such as a guitar or keyboard.

4

Treble Clef

A *clef* is at the beginning of each line of music. The *treble clef*, also called the *G clef*, shows that the second line is the note G.

Notes on the Staff

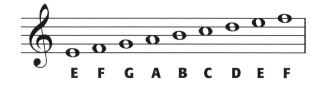

E F G A B C D E F

Notes are named using the first seven letters of the alphabet (A B C D E F G).

The notes on the lines are:

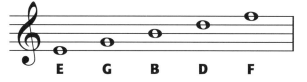

E G B D F

An easy way to remember this is the phrase "**E**very **G**ood **B**oy **D**oes **F**ine."

The notes in the spaces are:

F A C E

The way to remember this is the word **FACE**.

The staff can be extended to include even higher or lower notes by using *ledger lines*. This book uses the notes C and D below the bottom line of the staff.

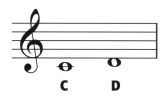

C D

In this book, every note has the note name inside of it to make playing the songs easier.

Measure
Music is divided into equal parts called *measures*.

Bar Lines
A *bar line* indicates where one measure ends and another begins.

Double Bar
A *double bar line*, made of one thin line and one thick line, shows the end of a piece of music.

Accidentals

An *accidental* raises or lowers the sound of a note. A *sharp* ♯ raises a note one half step. A *flat* ♭ lowers a note one half step. A *natural* ♮ cancels a sharp or flat. An accidental affects that note for the rest of that measure.

Fermata

A *fermata* ⌢ over a note means to hold it about twice as long as usual.

Ties

A *tie* is a curved line that joins two or more notes of the same pitch. Instead of playing the second note, continue to hold for the combined note value.

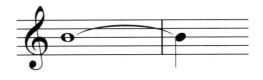

Hold for 5 beats.

Time Signature

4 = 4 beats to a measure
4 = quarter note ♩ gets 1 beat

6 = 6 beats to a measure
8 = eighth note ♪ gets 1 beat

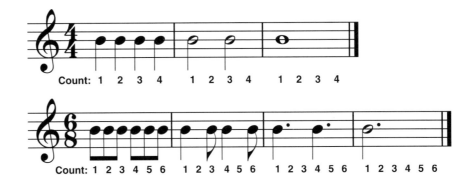

Repeat Signs

Go back to the beginning and play again.

Go back to the repeat sign and play again.

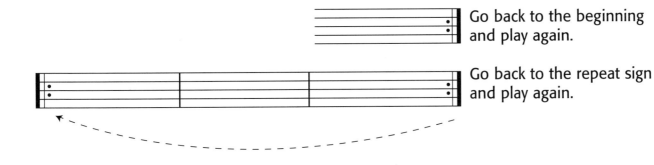

1st & 2nd Endings

Play the 1st ending the first time, repeat, then skip the 1st ending and play the 2nd ending.

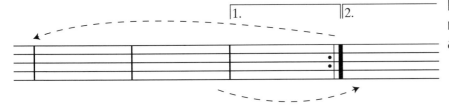

D.C. al Coda

Go back to the beginning and play to the coda sign (⊕), then skip to the coda to end the piece.

Let's Start Playing

Here are the notes you need to play Beethoven's "Ode to Joy." All of these notes are played with your left hand.

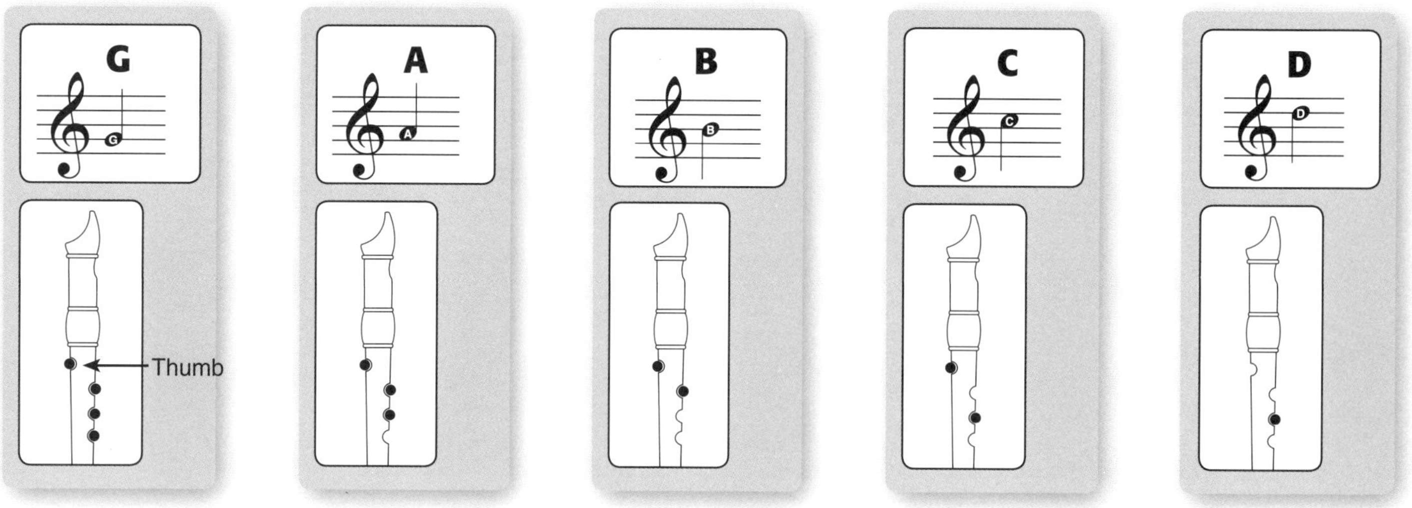

Remember: a quarter note ♩ gets 1 beat, and a half note 𝅗𝅥 gets 2 beats. Keep the beats even.

Ode to Joy

Ludwig van Beethoven

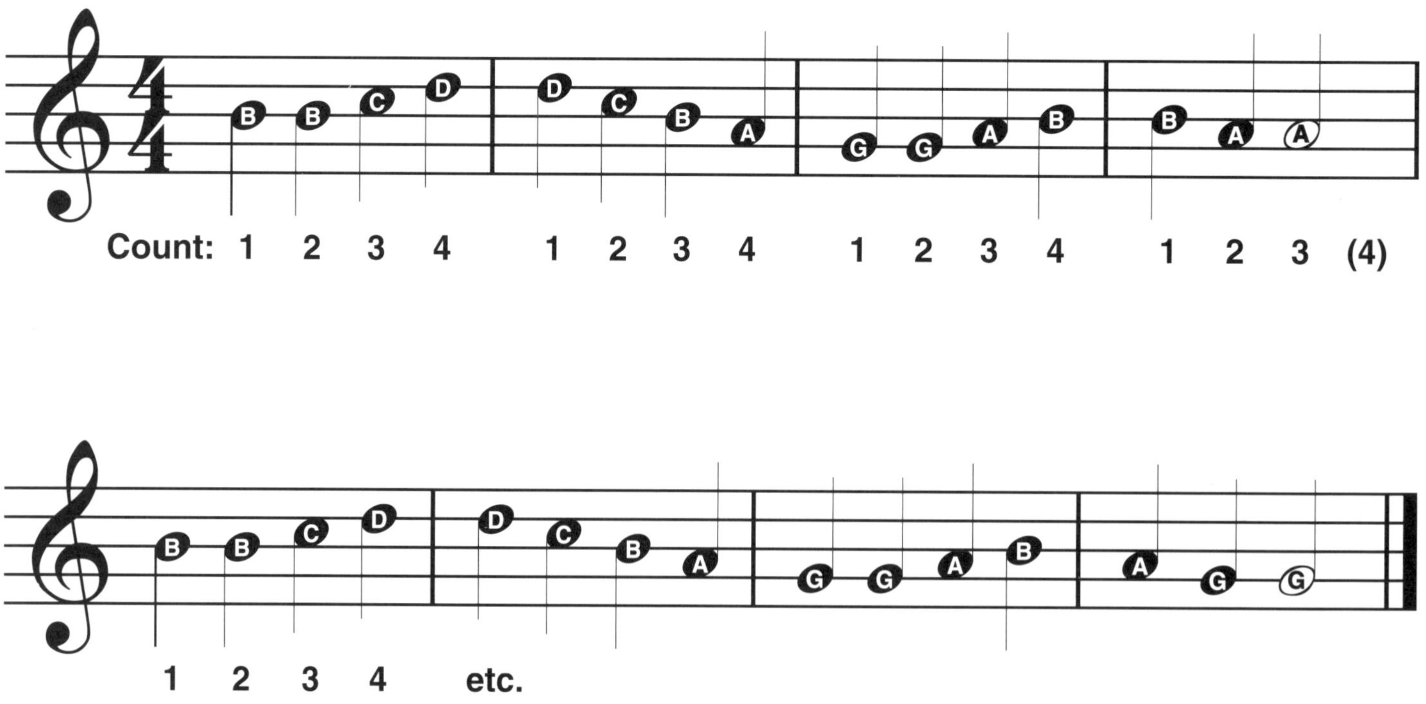

Adding Your Right Hand

For "Alouette," you will use your right hand to finger the note D.

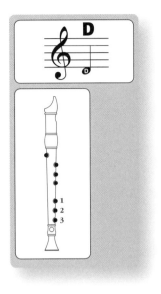

Remember: a whole note o gets 4 beats, and a quarter rest ⅃ gets 1 beat of silence.

Alouette

French folk song

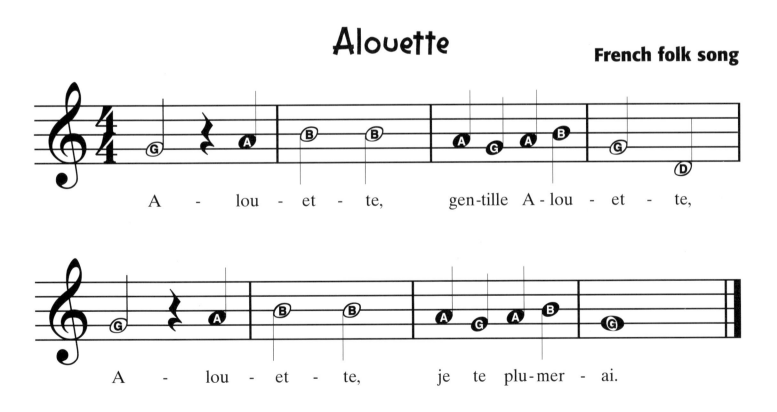

Complete Fingering Chart

● Closed Hole

◡ Partially Closed Hole

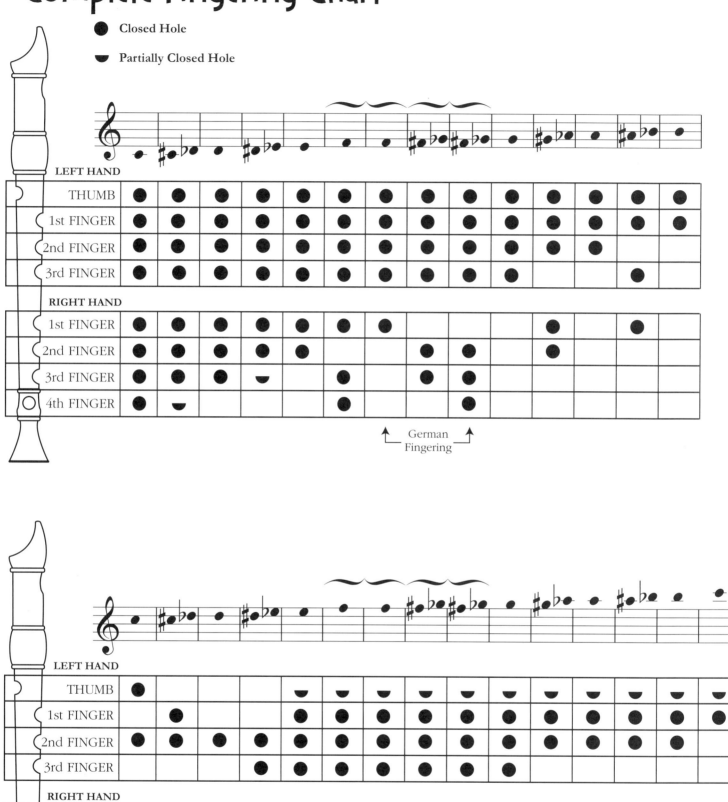

STAR WARS
(Main Theme)

Music by
JOHN WILLIAMS

Majestically

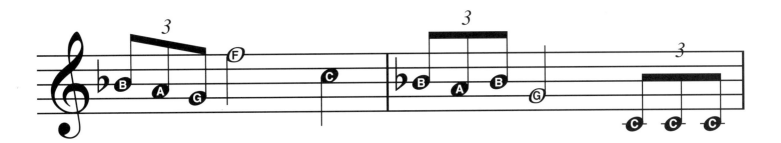

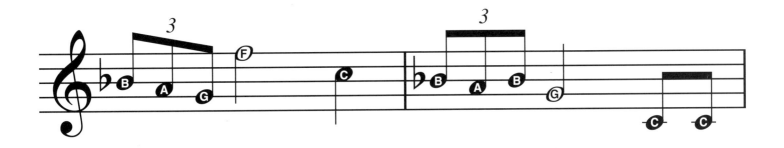

Star Wars - 3 - 1
30320

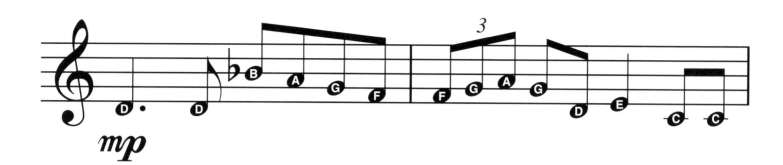

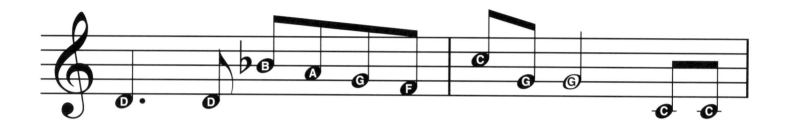

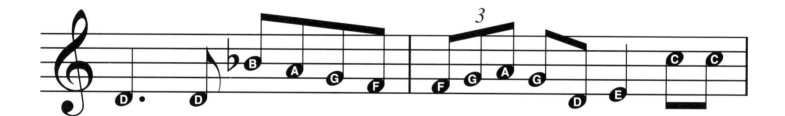

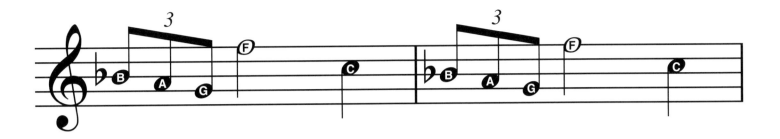

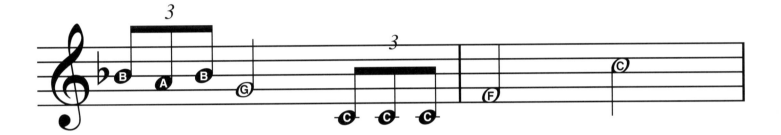

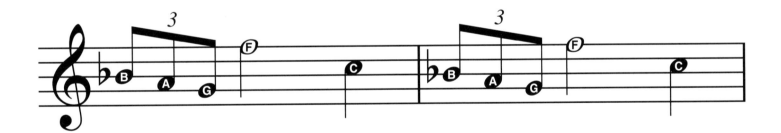

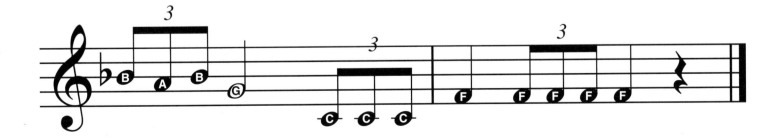

MAY THE FORCE BE WITH YOU

("The Force Theme")

By
JOHN WILLIAMS

Moderately

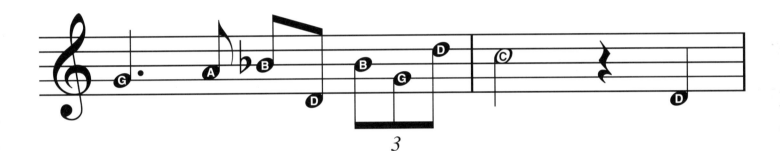

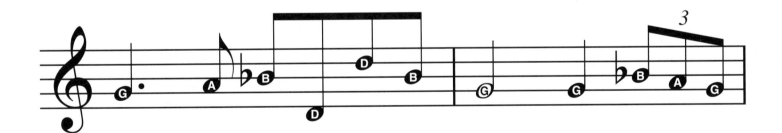

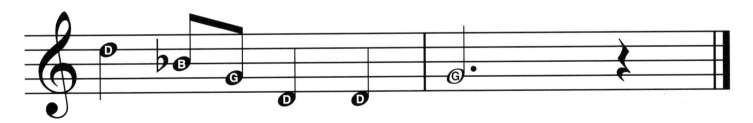

30320

THE IMPERIAL MARCH
("Darth Vader's Theme")

By
JOHN WILLIAMS

March

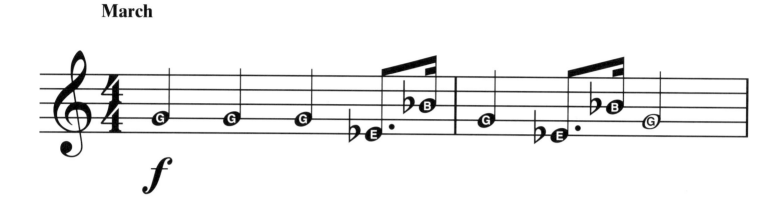

The Imperial March - 2 - 1
30320

The Imperial March - 2 - 2
30320

PRINCESS LEIA'S THEME

Music by
JOHN WILLIAMS

Slowly, with a gentle flow

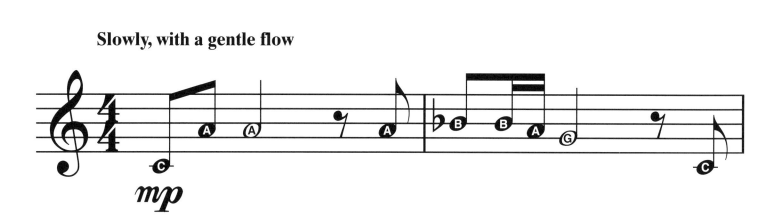

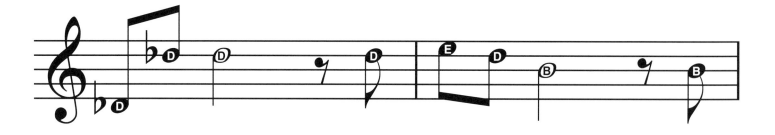

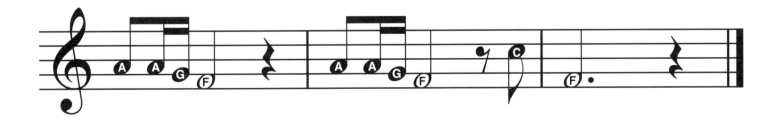

Princess Leia's Theme - 2 - 2
30320

DUEL OF THE FATES

By
JOHN WILLIAMS

Maestoso, with great force

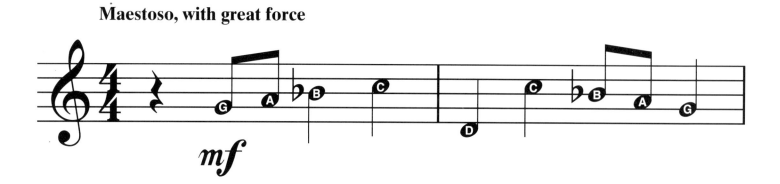

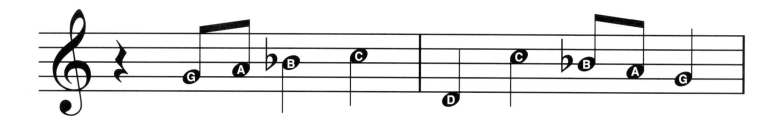

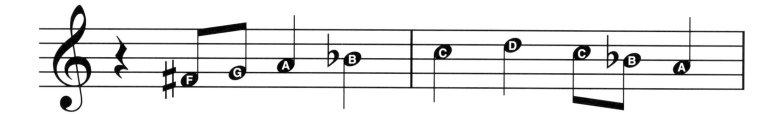

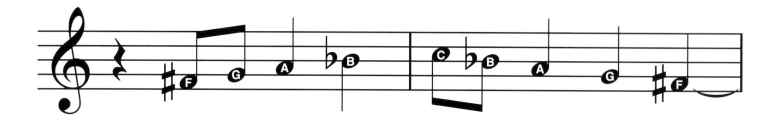

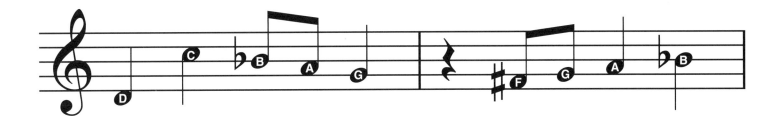

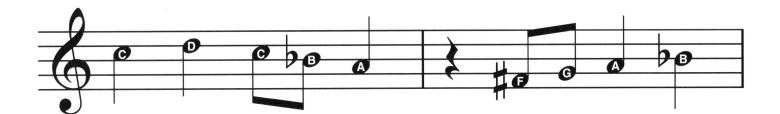

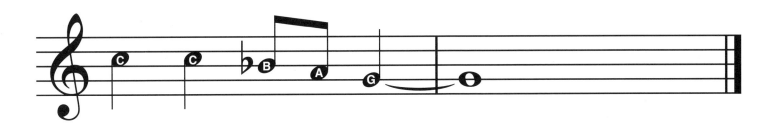

YODA'S THEME

By
JOHN WILLIAMS

Moderately

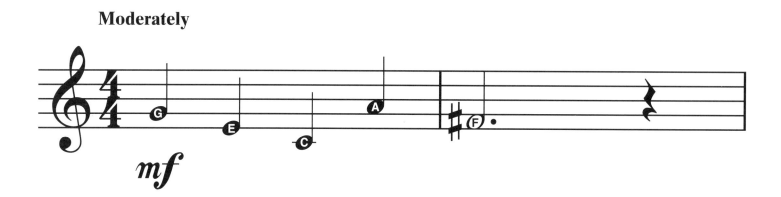

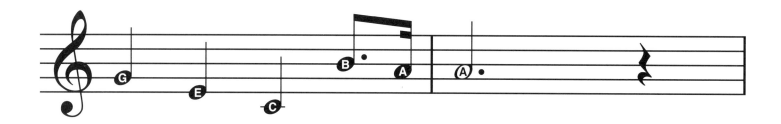

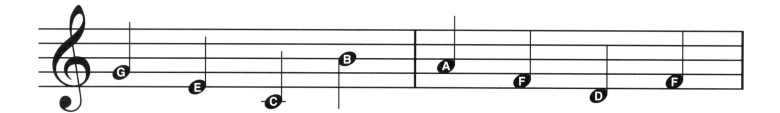

Yoda's Theme - 2 - 1
30320

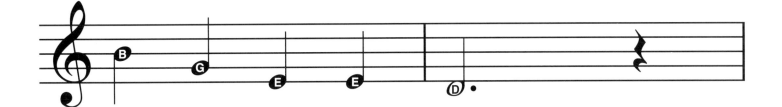

THE THRONE ROOM
(and End Title)

Music by
JOHN WILLIAMS

Maestoso

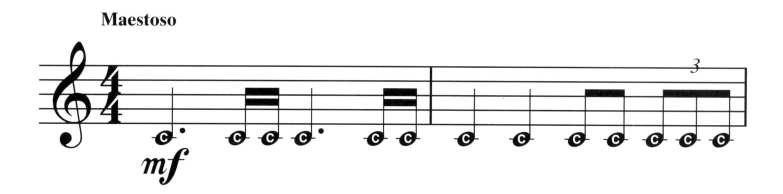

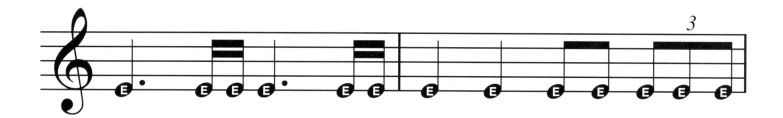

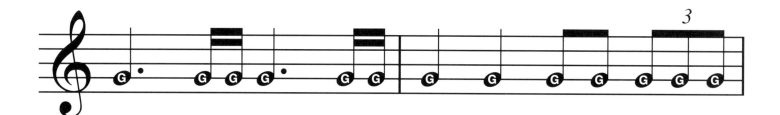

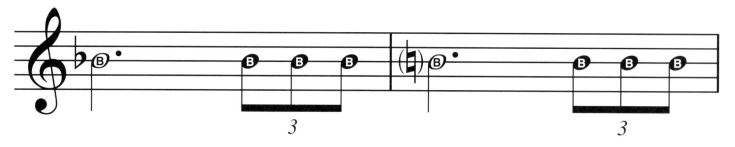

The Throne Room - 2 - 1
30320

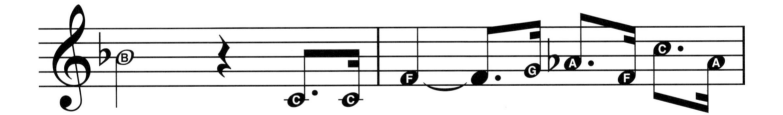

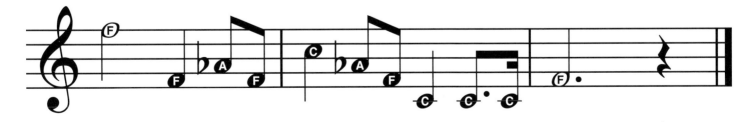

The Throne Room - 2 - 2
30320